These Lips

By Julie Cwir

Copyright © 2021 by Julie Cwir
First Edition printed independently by Julie Cwir in 2014
www.iwishidknown.yolasite.com

Text by Julie Cwir
Illustrations by Olga Egorova

All rights reserved. The use of any part of this publication reproduced, transmitted in any form or by any means, electronic, mechanical, photocopying, recording, or otherwise, or stored in a retrieval system, without the prior written consent of the author/publisher is an infringement of the copyright law.

ISBN: 9798767828845
Independently published with Kindle Direct Publications

This Book Belongs To

Our Brave Little Oscar
— ♡ —

These Lips are perfect in every way

No matter what others may say

These Lips are heaven sent

Perfected, just as they were meant

These Lips

are given tender

loving care

Because of the cleft that is beautiful and rare

These Lips have been given
many a kiss

But that wide smile is what
Mommy will miss

These Lips are my honor badge

That the surgeon will cut
to reattach

These Lips will endure much pain

The tears may fall down like rain

These Lips have been healed

The gap is now sealed

These Lips created a courage in me

I am the person I want to be

So, do not worry

There is nothing wrong

I am just

SIMPLY

POSITIVELY

ABSOLUTELY

Julie Cwir is an experienced self-published author. Her uplifting cleft story books include *I Wish I'd Known... How Much I'd Love You* and *I Wish I'd Known Clefts Create Courage*. Music and songwriting is her jam. She loves playing around with her 3 young boys, telling them adventurous bedtime stories and singing them to sleep.

Printed in Great Britain
by Amazon